1

NAKED WORDS 2.0

THE EFFECTIVE 157-WORD EMAIL

ISBN 978-0-9963893-4-1

***

Editor:
Divya Lavanya

***

***

***

***

Legal Disclaimer: Strategies and tips are only recommendations by this author; reading this book does not guarantee that your results will mirror my own results. This author cannot be held responsible for any unintentional errors or omissions that may be found in this book.

***

Please note: This entire book refers to marketing e-mails; e-mails that are supposed to get the recipient to do something – become interested in your product(s), service(s), or provide an answer or service. These days the majority of e-mails are marketing e-mails; we are either trying to sell products, services, or build our image (for instance at dating websites or for job applications).

***

Many thanks to CreateSpace for granting permission to reprint the e-mail featured in the chapter 'EXAMPLE OF A PERFECT E-MAIL'. This book is not endorsed by or affiliated with CreateSpace or Amazon.

***

***

***

A guide to concise, commanding communiques
Mary Vinnedge, **SUCCESS Magazine**

***

"In today's hectic world email is still the most direct way to share your message. *Naked Words* is a fantastic book that will show you how to get your message read and acted on."

Brian Burns, Host of **"The Brutal Truth About Sales & Selling"**-PodCast

***

"Naked Words 2.0 is the book to read if you want to maximize your chances of getting media features, sponsorships, or any other type of opportunity. If an employee is looking to advance their career or an entre-preneur is looking to build rapport with influencers, their next step should be buying this book."

Kallen Diggs, **International Bestselling Author & Huffington Post Columnist**

***

Table of Contents

***

3 STATEMENTS ABOUT COMMUNICATION

Please take a few seconds to reflect on the following three statements:

1. Any company or organization's best communicator is among its most valuable employees. On the list of greatest communicators in history are innovator and entrepreneur Steve Jobs, US president Ronald Reagan, and Civil Rights Leader Martin Luther King. We bought into their visions, ideas, and products because of their words.

2. E-mail has replaced the formal business letter.

3. Most likely you have to write e-mails daily. Make them count!

WHY IS THIS BOOK TITLED 'NAKED WORDS'?

This book's mission is to help you write better or best e-mails.

It presents facts, examples, and the unspoken rules.

It also includes twenty-seven e-mails, whose writers never thought about what the recipients would think when receiving these meaningless, silly, or even outright stupid messages; but that is what matters.

We write e-mails to help the recipients, to give them information, or to make them happy.

WHY SHOULD YOUR E-MAIL HAVE 157 WORDS?

It's a metaphor.

157 is a prime number. A prime number is a natural number greater than 1 that has no positive divisors other than 1 and itself. In other words, it is not pieced together, it is unique.

To stand out among the crowd of e-mails, your e-mails need to be as unique as prime numbers, which are special among the never-ending sequence of numbers.

Since most of us receive hundreds of messages daily, e-mails need to be short and concise to be effective. People get lost when reading too long e-mails; whenever they can, they skip them or delete them. When readers receive long e-mails, they quite often think

- If you can't say what you want in a few lines, don't expect me to find out!
- I don't have time for this, I have stuff to do!
- I expected an e-mail, not a novel.

On the other end of the spectrum, e-mails can be too short. An e-mail is NOT a text message. When people receive e-mails that show no effort, their reaction tends to be

- If you don't want to work on your own behalf, why should I? (=> 'delete')

E-mails of approximately 150 words can be read without having to scroll; the reader can grasp the content quickly and will more likely respond. Short, concise e-mails evoke the feeling that the sender is a competent and capable person.

You can easily test this effect by sending two e-mails to yourself, one with about 150 words and another one with about 300 words. Open them one after the other and observe *your emotions* when you just look at the e-mail (before you would begin to read).

Additionally, establishing a good contact means that the recipient will be interested in reading your future e-mails. You can present your agenda in small bites/short e-mails.

E-mails with approximately 150 words are appealing.

EXAMPLE OF A PERFECT E-MAIL

***

Hello Gisela,

Thank you for contacting us.

I understand you would like us to retire "Writing Great E-mails is Not Art - 9 Ways to get there," title ID 4793023.

I can confirm that your title is now retired in our system, which means that it is unavailable for production of new orders. However, your Amazon detail page will remain active as this listing information may persist to support activities such as sales of used copies through the Amazon Marketplace.

As you may know, Amazon offers customers the opportunity to find out-of-print books through their Marketplace. This is similar to a used bookstore as it is their aim to list a wide selection of titles for their customers' reference and convenience.

If you would like to un-retire your title, please use the Contact Us feature in your account to submit your request.

I hope this information proves helpful.

Merry Christmas!

Best regards,
(name)
CreateSpace Member Services*

***

Why is this e-mail great?

1) Friendly, personal greeting
2) Name of recipient is spelled correctly
3) Confirmation that the sender has understood my request
4) Confirmation that the sender has handled the request
5) Inclusion of important information
6) Short sectioned paragraphs that make it easy to grasp the content
7) Seasonal ending salutation

Could you feel that the sender did his best to help? Did you enjoy reading this e-mail?

It has 156 words; that is as close to 157 words as you can get.

The sender, CreateSpace, is a member of the Amazon group of companies. Amazon ranks #2 (only behind Apple, Inc.) on Fortune Magazine' list of Most Admired (companies) 2014.

* Many thanks to CreateSpace for granting permission to reprint this e-mail. This book is not endorsed by or affiliated with CreateSpace or Amazon.

WHAT ABOUT IF IT IS IMPOSSIBLE TO PRESENT YOUR MESSAGE IN ABOUT 150 WORDS?

GET CREATIVE! Attach a spreadsheet, a pdf document, a video, or provide a link to your website!

The Great Recession has led to hundreds of independent contractors offering their services on the worldwide web, from shooting videos to creating spreadsheets. Take advantage of this great pool of talent. Personally, I recommend Fiverr.com but depending on your location you may find great help at Craigslist or other websites.

IMPORTANT PSYCHOLOGICAL FACTORS

By nature humans appreciate drama. In a way we are internally programmed to like anticipation and suspense. We not only like dramatic books and movies but we also like the way we used to receive the mail.

For hundreds of years our ancestors had to wait for it. During the days of the Pony Express, letters might have even had a bullet hole.

[Image of a postal cover (mail) carried by the Pony Express which was stolen during a Piaute Indian raid. It was recovered two years later and made it to its destination in St. Joseph, Missouri. Notation on cover reads **"recovered from a mail stolen by the Indians in 1860"** *and bears a New York backstamp of May 3, 1862, the date when it was finally delivered in New York.]*

Try to compare that with the flood of e-mails we receive today without asking for it.

In the past days there was a process to receiving and consuming the news. People would judge the envelope and try to guess what kind of news it held. A foreign stamp could raise the expectations sky-high. A black-edged envelope was an ominous forewarning that somebody had died. An envelope with a pretty, golden imprint meant that somebody had gotten married or had a baby. Additionally, slicing the envelope open with a paper knife radiated a certain feeling of power, the sound of paper tearing added drama. There is no excitement in opening an e-mail.

One could make a case that we receive more 'stuff' than ever, but the way it is delivered is less exciting than ever; consequently, the words have become more important.

MINDBOGGLING STATISTICS

Worldwide over 100 billion e-mails are sent every day. The Radicati Group, Inc, a Technology Market Research Firm forecasts that by the end of 2017 over 132 billion e-mails will be sent and received per day. Workers spend about 11.2 hours or 28% of their workweek dealing with e-mails.

This leads to the obvious question: "How do you create an e-mail that stands out among the crowd, the immense crowd?"

The simple answer to this question is, "Your e-mail needs to have the same impact as if you had a short meeting in person with the recipient."

Please read this sentence again and reflect on it: Your e-mail needs to have the same impact as if you had a short meeting in person with the recipient.

For every vague 'blah blah' e-mail, there is a concise, meaningful, and beautiful e-mail. Considering the flood of e-mails and information all of us receive, we have to make decision on whose e-mails we read and whose e-mails we delete. Most of us also form an opinion about people who keep sending 'blah blah' e-mails.

THE PROBLEM WITH TEMPLATES

Some people search for templates on the Internet. There is also a saying, "you know you are trouble when your search leads you to page 2 on google," meaning that most people use the information they find on page 1 of their Google search.

These days very often 100+ people apply for the same job. Can you imagine how many almost identical cover letters human resources experts get to see simply because a majority of people picked the same template?

However, it needs to be stated that the problem isn't that people use a template, the problem is that too many people use the *same* templates.

Naturally you don't want to create the same content over again, when you apply for more than one job, or if you send a marketing or sales email to many clients. The best way to go is to create your own original template, and work with this "personal template."

You know everything about the product, including if the

product is you, because you want to apply for a job or a promotion.

There is no template for expressing the desire to succeed.

THE 7 PARTS OF AN E-MAIL

After I published "Naked Words: The Effective 157-Word Email" in March 2015 a few readers were a bit sad to find out that I did not publish a "magic bullet" or "magic template(s)."

To help with this situation I published "NAKED WORDS 2.0", which you are holding in your hands. It includes action steps you can take, as well as more examples of the good and the not so good. These samples are purposely short, they are building blocks instead of templates.

The simple truth is that templates are easily detected in today's ever-connected world; for instance, this book is being sold all around the world.

In the 21st century, templates are the death of successful marketing.

Today, people compete for business or jobs with people from their hometown, different US states, and even the whole world.

Therefore, only your very own unique e-mail, which you composed yourself, will

- stand out of the crowd,
- represent your brand, and
- be a marketing tool for YOU.

Even technical or legal e-mails are marketing tools, in a way.

A real estate agent who works with a new closing attorney forms an opinion about the closing attorney's work when reading his e-mails. Since quite often real estate agents are asked to recommend a closing attorney, every closing attorney's e-mail serves also as a marketing brochure. Will a real estate agent recommend an attorney, whose employees send incomplete, late, or somewhat impolite e-mails? Probably not, because such a recommendation will reflect badly onto the person who made the recommendation.

In his groundbreaking book "Purple Cow: Transform Your Business by Being Remarkable," famed marketing guru Seth Godin makes a clear case for "To be noticed, a product has to be remarkable."

E-mails should be remarkable too.

An e-mail created from a template can never be a magic e-mail.

There is only one kind of magic e-mail – the one you create – from scratch.

You and your product are unique. You are your own brand; you have your own style. Your e-mails should support both.

Here is an analogy from a different field: the world of movies. Actors have to audition for movie roles. Not only movie stars, but all actors who are supposed to do more than "standing around in the background" have to audition.

For instance, a movie script might ask for thirty extras who know how to dance the tango. Typically, ten to twenty times as many actors will audition.

During the audition process, the prospective extras will wait for their turn to show off their dancing skills, lined up in a queue in a waiting room (just like e-mails are lined up in the recipient's Inbox), till finally each one gets his turn.

Most e-mails get their turn too, even if only eventually.

But, there is more to an audition than selecting actors for *specific* roles. At the same time while the director is checking on the dancing skills of the extras, he also looks at them as actors, aside from being extras who know how to dance the tango. The director may decide that an auditioning actor may be perfect for another part, maybe even for a speaking role, or for his next movie. Equally everybody forms an opinion about the senders of the e-mails they receive.

In fact, this has happened to me. When in the past I applied for a job the company's vice president called me to tell me that they would like to offer me a different position, one that was not even advertised. It is for this reason that you should never use a template when penning an e-mail.

In the world of movies "performances based on templates" get to hear "NEEEXT!"

In the world of e-mails, "e-mails based on templates" most often get deleted.

Please note:

Throughout this book, the pronoun "he" is used with intended gender-neutral meaning, as "he" has been used traditionally in English. Whenever you read "he," I could be referring to a man or woman. Unless noted otherwise, I protect the privacy of others, which in this book includes not even revealing the person's gender.

The depicted avatars are a visualization of the same concept. The avatars too are to be understood with intended gender-neutral meaning, as "he" has been used traditionally in English.

Please also note: The featured e-mails are 'based' on true e-mails.

#1 –THE SENDER'S (YOUR) NAME

Like many of you, I still remember the very first e-mail I received in 1998. Then, hardly any of my friends had a computer. Fascinated, I read every e-mail and every newsletter I received. Today it's a whole new ballgame. Like most of us I slowly move my mouse over the column with the names of senders, read the names, and delete e-mails, three times per day. Quite many of the 100 billion e-mails that are being sent every day find their way into my Inbox. Nobody reads all their e-mails anymore.

The most important part of any e-mail is its sender's name. We care mostly about the e-mails from people we like or from people who are significant in our lives.

We also spend more time addressing the ideas, thoughts, and wishes from people who we consider important to us. At the same time all of us delete e-mails without ever looking at any other information than the sender's name.

Luckily, in life we get hundreds of chances to create a name for ourselves and to build our reputation.

From 2000 – 2002, I taught a freshman class called "Careers" at a high school in South Florida. This was a nine-week course, created to teach high school students how to apply for a job. Every nine weeks between 29 and 33 new students walked into my classroom; since they were freshmen, I did not know any of them.

On the first day of the course, I told my new students that I had no intention to find out if any of them had had pulled a silly prank in middle school; I also did not care who their sibling was, they would be in charge of building their own reputation in my class.

Naturally, since I taught four of these courses per year, I had a hard time remembering the students' names. I told them that and also, "You don't want to be the first student whose name I remember, unless you are aiming for being the best student in this class."

All of us remember the remarkable and the outstanding first, the good and the bad.

Of course, two weeks after the course started, I knew all of my students' names. But, what about – today?

There are about a dozen students whose work I still remember – clearly and in detail. Even fifteen years later, I know what projects these students presented, how they scored, and should one of them, a student with the initials AW, ever run for president, I'll be the first one to say, "I knew it then!"

Considering that all of us receive many more than 120 e-mails from new contacts per year, it is not quite the same in the world of e-mails. Still, when we look at the names of people who send us e-mails, all of us have an immediate association with the sender's work, attitude, personal qualities, and anything else the sender volunteered.

Today, becoming that person, whose e-mail everybody will open first is called brand-building. Everybody has to do it himself.

That includes protecting your name! Think long and hard before you associate your name with an organization you don't really know.

[*Obviously, all of us need to venture out and discover new social media platforms, websites, online clubs etc. However, in the interest of protecting your name, I recommend not to invite your valuable business contacts to new platforms before you know how useful, interesting, and/or practical these venues are. You can always invite your contacts later, once you know more about a new social media platform.*

Besides, you don't need to engage in marketing any new organizations. If they are remarkable, all of us will hear about them sooner or later. Even my grandmother knew about Facebook.]

ACTION STEPS:

- Obviously, you are the only one who can make your name so special that every recipient wants to open your e-mail first – you create and represent *your brand*. If you do it well you will be able to reap the benefits for a long time.

- Define your brand! It does not matter whether you are a budding rock star or the best closing attorney in a small city; your attire, your way of communicating, as well as your way of writing e-mails should support your brand. While a budding rock star could use the ending salutation "Don't Stop Believing, (name)", inspired by the title of an anthem by the American rock band Journey, this would be a totally inappropriate ending salutation for a closing attorney.

- Do not pester people with irrelevant, boring, story-of-yesterday messages. Everybody knows where the 'delete-key' is.

- If you don't know the recipient personally, consider calling him/her first, so you can introduce yourself and start building rapport before you send that first e-mail. Calling first also signals real interest as opposed to lazily sending a mass e-mail. (Anybody can do that and all recipients know it.) Then again, if you are able to create interest during a phone conversation, the recipient will look for your e-mail, which gives you an advantage with respect to your e-mail's positioning in the recipient's Inbox.

#2 – THE BEST TIME TO SEND AN E-MAIL

Fast & timely – electronic communication is supposed to happen fast!

Unfortunately, it is a fact that most people do not bother to answer an e-mail to which they do not have all the answers. They wait until they have the answers and only then reply. Therefore, this is a great opportunity for you to shine and stand out among the crowd.

A few pages back I stated "Your e-mail needs to have the same impact as if you had a short meeting – in person – with the recipient." Let's assume for a minute that a business partner had made a certain request during a personal meeting instead of via e-mail. Right away you would answer, "Thanks, (name), for the opportunity to handle this request for you. My team and I will get to work right away. You can expect an answer/quote/offer in about four to five days."

[You would not stand there quietly and say nothing because you plan on replying when you have all information. Yet, that is exactly how many people handle e-mail requests.]

Replying with a quick e-mail is a great way to strengthen your relationship with your business partners.

"Dear (name), Thank you for inquiring about/ requesting ...xyz... Though I do not have all answers/ numbers/ information yet, my team and I are already working on it. I will be in touch as soon as I have more information. In the meantime, please feel free to contact me with any questions or updates you might have. As always, (signature)"

Replying in a timely manner is a fabulously easy way to build your brand. By doing so, you are attaching the attribute 'reliable' to your name.

ACTION STEP:

- Always acknowledge the receipt of every important e-mail within six hours.

#3 – THE ATTRACTIVE & EFFECTIVE SUBJECT LINE

To illustrate the importance of a great subject line I am going to use the example of our casting director again. Let's assume, our casting director has been looking at extras who are supposed to play various office employees for hours. Getting hungry and tired he decides to take a peek at the next few candidates. He looks through a window in the door and sees only the lower body parts of the next group of actors. Our director cannot see the "content," the expressive faces of the actors.

Of course, the director does not know if any of these actors are great actors, but immediately he will form an opinion about whether these actors are confident, bored, or want to stand out like the woman with the orange folder.

While all of us would judge that the man on the left is bored, that the woman with the orange folder is trying to get attention in every possible way, and that the man in the middle appears to be extra confident, maybe even cocky, who do we NOT notice at first glance?

[It's the same for e-mails.]

After taking a preliminary peek at the actors, our director's opinion would be influenced. Probably he would pay more attention to the performance of the woman with the orange folder than to the performances of the other women. Naturally, that does not mean that she gets the part BUT in the world of e-mails the recipient would open the "orange e-mail" **first**.

In the world of e-mails subject lines "audition" for getting opened first.

Therefore, make your subject line stand out! In the "world of marketing e-mails" standing out leads to getting read first, which can make the difference for your proposal.

Again, every situation is different. If you work in the computer industry and you are in the position to write into the subject line, "CEO Tim Cook suggested that I get in touch with you..." that is what you should write.

In the absence of such an opportunity, putting any number into the subject line will make YOUR subject line stand out like the woman with the orange folder.

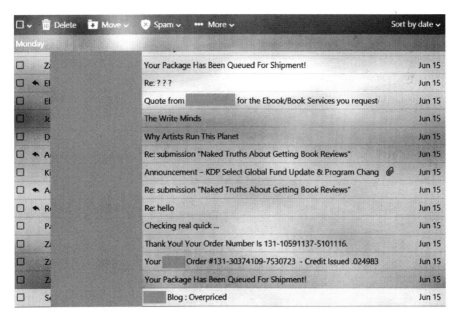

Looking at this screen print of my Inbox you probably notice how the subject lines with order numbers stand out. You can create the same effect for any kind of e-mail.

Naturally, creative business and/or marketing e-mails ask for a different type of subject line than technical and legal e-mails. Most often business and/or marketing e-mails are written to sell something and therefore need to be exciting. Technical and/or legal e-mails are to inform and therefore need to give precise information.

Still, the following rule will improve any kind of e-mails:

Use a number in your subject line, ANY number!

Numbers attract attention. Marketing people have known this for a while as the following examples demonstrate:

- "We'll handle 33% faster or 20% cheaper"

- "$5.55 off" or even

- "Meeting at 2:00 p.m.!"

Numbers are also the best way to relate technical or legal information as the following examples demonstrate:

- Purchase order 123456/2014 with expected shipping date 04/04/2014

- Doe v. Doe, 100 Ohio St.2d 345, 2013-Ohio-2419 and even

- Meeting Minutes 1/2/2015, 10:00 AM, CEO Mr. Robert Smith & Marketing Dept.

Consequently, to make your e-mail more effective, put a number into your subject line! There are prices, percentages, quantities, dates/times, street numbers, and even temperatures.

- We are expecting temperatures in the low 20's – Does your heater work?

Additionally, the effective subject line is also an opportunity to show off manners and style. Both are managerial qualities. For example, the subject line

- Meeting Minutes 1/2/2015, 10:00 AM, CEO Mr. Robert Smith & Marketing Dept.

demonstrates that the writer is a thorough, organized, as well as a polite person.

If it is customary at your company to use e-mail threads (the original e-mail with a running list of all subsequent replies), always check the subject line for inaccuracies. It is another great way to show off perfect e-mail writing skills. If somebody else started the e-mail and the subject line does not contain the relevant number or topic => Change it! Make yourself a valuable player in this conversation, though you should not delete the original subject line. That would show disrespect.

Example:

Original e-mail's subject line: case Robert Smith, Pennsylvania Ave

Improved e-mail: **Case# 123456** *case Robert Smith, Pennsylvania Ave

Now, let's look again at my Inbox

☐ ⌄	🗑 Delete	📁 Move ⌄	✖ Spam ⌄ ••• More ⌄	Sort by date ⌄

Monday

☐	Z.	Your Package Has Been Queued For Shipment!	Jun 15
☐ ↰	E	Re: ? ? ?	Jun 15
☐	E	Quote from ▨▨▨▨ for the Ebook/Book Services you request	Jun 15
☐	Jc	The Write Minds	Jun 15
☐	D	Why Artists Run This Planet	Jun 15
☐ ↰	A	Re: submission "Naked Truths About Getting Book Reviews"	Jun 15
☐	Ki	Announcement – KDP Select Global Fund Update & Program Chang 📎	Jun 15
☐ ↰	A	Re: submission "Naked Truths About Getting Book Reviews"	Jun 15
☐ ↰	R	Re: hello	Jun 15
☐	P	Checking real quick ...	Jun 15
☐	Z	Thank You! Your Order Number Is 131-10591137-5101116.	Jun 15
☐	Z	Your ▨▨▨ Order #131-30374109-7530723 - Credit Issued .024983	Jun 15
☐	Z	Your Package Has Been Queued For Shipment!	Jun 15
☐	Sc	▨▨ Blog : Overpriced	Jun 15

What do you think about the e-mail with the subject line "Re: hello"?

Are you bewildered? At least I was when I saw it. This could not possibly be a reply to one of my e-mails. As an e-mail evangelist, I would never put the word "hello" into a subject line.

Consequently, the letters "Re:", which indicate a reply, couldn't have been created automatically by the sender's e-mail program.

It turned out that the sender tried to trick me by putting "Re:" into the subject line, probably so I would open his e-mail faster and not delete it. Trickery is not welcome, anywhere. So, I blocked the sender. I would recommend that you consider doing the same should you receive a similar e-mail.

However, I did write "? ? ?" into a subject line. I purposely selected this type of subject line to get the recipient's immediate attention in regards to a problem; I also happen to know the recipient very well. (Please note: the "Do-Not-Cry-Wolf" rule applies. Most everybody will blacklist or block people who abuse this trick.)

ACTION STEPS:

- In lieu of other eye-catching subject lines always put a number (order number, reference, number, date, time, price, percentage…) into the subject line.

- In emergencies, raise attention by putting special signs, question marks, or exclamation marks into the subject line.

- To test the effectiveness of subject lines for marketing e-mails, send e-mails of various options you are pondering to yourself. Close your Inbox. Walk away and get some distance. After that, open your Inbox again. You will probably see right away which subject line stands out.

- Create a folder in which you collect great subject lines from e-mails you receive. This collection is for your reference and inspiration. When in the future you cannot come up with an idea, you could use this list for inspiration.

#4 – THE GREETING

Greeting and salutation are another easy way to stand out among the crowd of e-mail writers. Having looked at over 100,000 e-mails, I can vouch for the fact that most people use the same greeting and salutation as the next writer and even the next.

If you find a way to express that you really care about the recipient, you have effectively elevated your e-mail over 90% of all other e-mails in your recipient's Inbox.

It is actually easier than one might think.

Picture yourself entering your office building in the morning. As you enter, you meet a colleague who says "Hi". Next, you meet a colleague who greets you with "Good morning, Pete. How is it going?" There is no need to explain. One of the people is interested in being in a business relationship with you, the other one is just doing enough to be polite.

With a bit of effort you can create the same experience via e-mail. Remember, the goal is to demonstrate that you truly care to be in business with the recipient, that you want to solve his problems (and get for paid for it), and that even if nothing shells out right now, you want to be in a business relationship, which may lead to mutual business endeavors in the future.

Examples of greetings that imply that the sender is interested in building a genuine business relationship

- "Good morning" (needs to be sent before 9:00 AM)

    indicates: "Your e-mail, respectively tending to your issues, is so important to me that I won't wait. I am taking care of this as the **first** thing in the morning."

- "(name), quickly before I leave...."

indicates: "Your agenda is so important to me that I **won't leave** my office before I tend to it…"

- "Good to hear from you, (name)!"

  [Write this only if you mean it. If you mean or think it – why not say so? People like to hear that somebody likes to hear from them.]

Clearly, writing **any** other greeting than "hi" will make your e-mail stand out. This one does too…

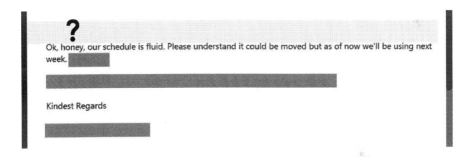

Ok, honey, our schedule is fluid. Please understand it could be moved but as of now we'll be using next week. ████

████████████████████████

Kindest Regards

██████████

[… though, 'honey' happens to be NOT on my list of preferred greetings.]

Better options are

- Dear

- Good Morning

- Good Afternoon

- Happy Holidays (Happy Easter, Happy Thanksgiving, etc.)

- Happy Spring Beginning!

- Greetings All (group e-mail)

- [Don't forget local holidays]

Also, consider thanking your recipient right away, in the first sentence of your e-mail. Most people work extremely hard and receive little thanks. Being the person who thanks them elevates you to becoming that special person whose e-mails everybody wants to open and read.

Here are the opening lines of an e-mail I wrote, which was very well received.

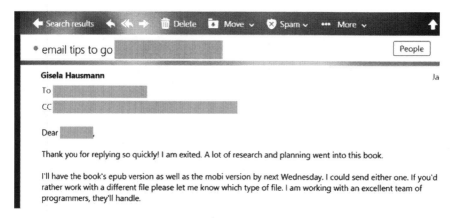

In a world where 100 billion e-mails are being sent every day, a quick response is something to be thankful for.

Notice how I raise the level of communication by writing, "I am excited." Expressing your feelings in a positive and professional tone will lead to your e-mails being more appealing than canned, pieced-together e-mails. Make an effort of doing it at the beginning of the e-mail.

Please also note that words 63 and 64 mention my "excellent team." Nobody can do everything on his own. Mentioning partners or your team creates a positive impression. If possible, do it at the beginning of the e-mail.

Even though I recommend avoiding using the greeting "hi," sometimes it can be the best option.

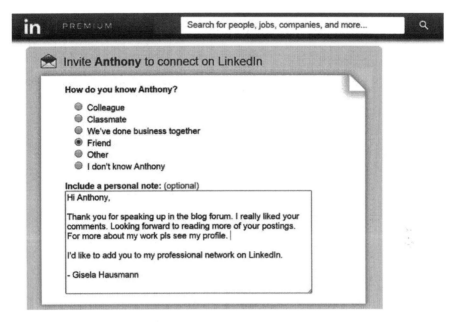

If you are contacting somebody on Linkedin your initial e-mail is limited to 400 characters. Under these circumstances "hi" is most likely the best greeting. Instead of skipping the "thank-you," you should elect to write "hi" because it takes up only two characters.

ACTION STEPS

- Select a best greeting

- Thank the recipient

- Make an effort to indicate that this e-mail exchange is important to you, that you care about the issue, and that you and your team are giving your best effort.

#5 – THE SPELLING OF THE RECIPIENT'S NAME

There is no faster way to say "I don't really care about you…" than misspelling a person's name. I learned this at the beginning of my career. Then, unusual names or unusual spellings of first names weren't as customary as they are today. At the time, I knew a lady by the name Britany. Of course, traditionally this name is spelled with two T's. However, Britany's parents had decided to give her name an unusual spin. One day, she and I were talking about a mutual business contact (let's call him Charlie) and Britany articulated her devastating verdict:

"Charlie doesn't care about anything. He cannot even get my name right, even though we have known each other for two years…"

This may sound as if Britany was in a huff but the truth is – she was completely right. Charlie did not pay attention because he did not care.

Typically, people who have an unusual name or whose name is spelled in an unusual way have to spell their name often; they learn to pay attention to little details. Consequently, they know that everybody who does not do that does not care.

If Charlie would only have known how sizeable Britany's marketing budget was, he might have learned to pay attention to the little details very quickly.

However, on rare occasions some people demonstrate an ability to correct this mishap and look even better than if they hadn't made the mistake. In this world of canned e-mails and automated responses we are looking for the human side in people. This e-mail writer endeared himself by showing that he cared.

To 'Gisela Hausmann'

Sorry Gisela,
I just saw I committed the cardinal sin of misspelling your name!

In today's world of international trade, it is crucial to pay closest attention to the spelling of foreign names. To avoid possible mistakes you might consider copying your business partner's name. To do this properly, you need to copy the person's name into a file that will strip any existing formatting (.txt). Only then paste the name from the .txt file into the e-mail. [All Microsoft Office programs keep the text's original formatting.]

The following e-mail illustrates the opposite process. In this case the sender copied and pasted the e-mail's body from a MS word document into his e-mail and then added my name manually. How do I know?

The e-mail features two different fonts. Since my name is misspelled, the sender could not have copied and pasted my name but had to have copied and pasted the body of the e-mail.

While the greeting ("Hello Gisella") is written in the font as defined by the sender's e-mail program settings, the body of the e-mail is displayed in a different font. This was caused by copying and pasting from a program that kept the original text's formatting.

On Thursday, February 1, 2015 11:05 AM,
<   > wrote:
Hello Gisella,

Firstly let me introduce myself. My name is   and I'm a Writer, Blogger and

Making this mistake is also one of the easiest ways for the recipient to find out that he received a mass e-mail.

Sending out e-mails that can be easily identified as mass e-mails invites the recipient to think, "I don't even need to consider this e-mail. Probably the sender sent the same e-mail to another 100 people. *Somebody else* is going to do it." => delete!

ACTION STEP

- Make sure to copy all texts into MS .txt or similar program before you paste it into an e-mail.

6 – THE BODY OF YOUR E-MAIL

Obviously, the content of e-mails can be vastly different, but the following three tips can be applied to all e-mails:

TIP 1: is probably the most important tip of this entire book: READ IMPORTANT E-MAILS OUT LOUD TO YOURSELF! At the beginning of this book I stated, 'Your e-mail needs to have the same impact as if you had a short meeting in person'. By reading your e-mail out loud, you are simulating that situation.

At this time I am challenging you to test the importance of this tip! Please open your sent-folder and read the last e-mail you sent to your boss out loud. Did you like it? Would you maybe change one word, or more?

TIP 2: Also, before sending very important e-mails, get some distance! Leave your desk! Go to the break room to get coffee or maybe take a stroll around the building. The idea is that you get your blood flowing and at the same time you clear your mind by looking at some different scenery. Then take a last look at your e-mail, read it out loud one more time, and only then, once you have re-verified that it is the best it can be, send it off!

TIP 3: If there is no need for the recipient to reply type "NNTR – No Need To Reply" at the bottom of the e-mail and above the signature. It signals that you value your recipient's time. He will appreciate that. This, too, is a way to build your brand as a cool and tech-savvy person.

Special consideration has to be given to the Direct Marketing E-mail

This type of e-mail could be considered cold-calling in the form of an e-mail; quite often it is done at social media platforms, for instance Linkedin. If done well it is an excellent way for industry professionals to introduce their business services.

The advantage of this method is that the sender, who wants to offer his service(s), can research the recipient's business on the Internet, and then tailor his e-mail to the needs of the potential client. The recipient's obvious advantage is that he can see whether the sender actually did that.

As an e-mail evangelist, I have high standards. One of the very best direct e-mails I ever received came from an ebook cover designer. It featured the following, very elegantly written lines:

**

"... *Branding the author* is imperative, the designer is responsible for presenting their image as a first impression to the public, special thought and time should go into font, color scheme and placement.

As a designer I feel that *hearing the heart of the story* from you, the author, your passion for your creation fuels my creativity and design process..."

**

Doesn't this e-mail sound great? The writer seems to address authors' (my) needs.

Still, I would not even open this designer's website and check out his work. That's because I know for a fact that this designer did not make the effort of clicking his mouse only once – to look at my website. This effort would have taken no longer than three seconds.

These are my books.

Would the sender of this e-mail have made the minimal effort of clicking on the link to my website, he would have seen these seven covers. He probably would not have sent me his 'canned e-mail', even though it is a masterfully written e-mail.

I already publish books under *my own brand of 'naked' books*; they are *non-fiction* books, and with the exception of one, they are *not story books*.

So, what *branding* and *hearing the story* was this designer referring to?

Quite obviously, he did not invest the minimal effort of clicking the link to my website but was fishing for business with his standard e-mail.

***

Obviously no book can address every possible issue, but if the senders of the following e-mails would have read their e-mails out loud, they probably would not have sent them.

RE: ▓▓▓▓▓▓▓▓▓▓▓▓

▓▓▓▓▓▓▓▓▓▓▓▓

May 21, 2012, 1:16 PM

You replied to this message:

Happy Monday !

Thank you so very much Gisela for sending me and sharing with me all of this exciting information.

I look forward to reviewing it all.

Keep up the fantastic work.

I look forward to your reply.

I'm wishing you an awesome work week too !

Sincerely, ▓▓▓▓▓▓▓▓▓▓

[*Hmm…*]

RE: Greetings

August 29, 2014, 3:08 PM

Hi, Gisela.
I didn't know that you'd moved to Greenville. I suppose that is in South Carolina?
That is a good area--excellent public library, and you have the A. Wyeth Museum--and Paris Mountain.
Furman University there is also a plus for the area...

On 08/28/14 1:32 PM, Gisela Hausmann wrote:

Hope you doing too,

How are you r various activities in Wilmington going?

Of course you have noticed that I have moved to Greenville, I enjoy the change in scenery. After living at the Eastern seaboard for 26 yrs, living close to the mountains is nice.

Ciao,

Glsela

[*Some e-mail writers seem to lose track of why they write an e-mail in the first place. In this case, a contact from my old hometown sent me a "reconnect"-email. Reading his first e-mail I suspected that he had not noticed that I had moved.*

Trying to be polite, I replied and presented this information as if I thought that he knew that I had moved.

To my utter surprise, he admitted that he did not know and elaborated on highlights of my new hometown. To this day, I have no idea why he wrote me.]

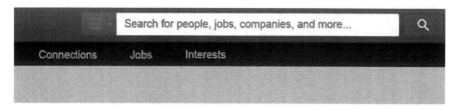

Inbox

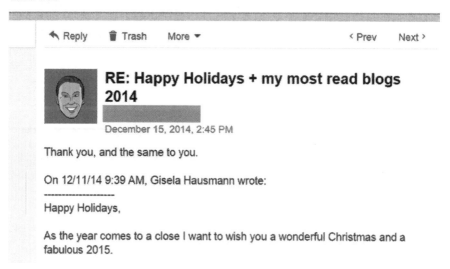

RE: Happy Holidays + my most read blogs 2014

December 15, 2014, 2:45 PM

Thank you, and the same to you.

On 12/11/14 9:39 AM, Gisela Hausmann wrote:

Happy Holidays,

As the year comes to a close I want to wish you a wonderful Christmas and a fabulous 2015.

[*Obviously this e-mail is well-meant.*

Besides being really short, the effort is a nice gesture. However, this e-mail represents a "missed opportunity." The sender missed to say something interesting, meaningful, or something nice.

To stay on recipients' priority list of people whose e-mails get opened first, e-mails need to present content.]

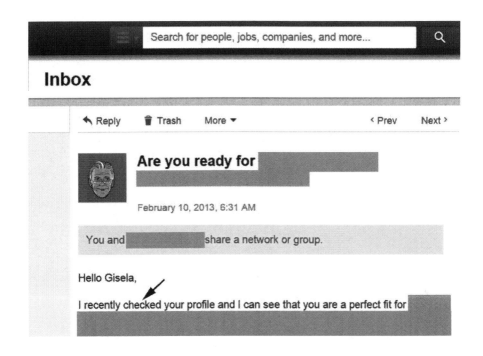

[This e-mail would have truly benefitted from reading it out loud. On a bad day, the opening sentence sounds outright creepy.]

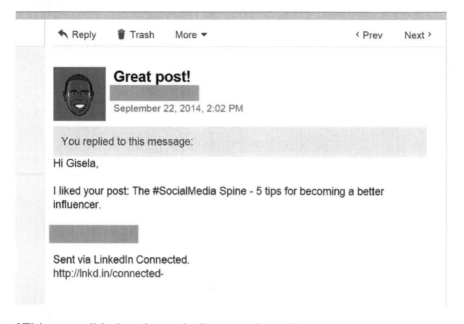

Reply   Trash   More ▾   ‹ Prev   Next ›

Great post!

September 22, 2014, 2:02 PM

You replied to this message:

Hi Gisela,

I liked your post: The #SocialMedia Spine - 5 tips for becoming a better influencer.

Sent via LinkedIn Connected.
http://lnkd.in/connected-

[*This e-mail is lovely and all around positive.*

Still, the sender missed a marketing opportunity for **himself***. Not always is sending an e-mail the very best option. Had the sender commented below the blog, I would have appreciated his compliment just the same; at the same time, the sender could have put out his name – for more people to see than just me. When people comment on a blog, they always get the opportunity to link to their own website.*]

ACTION STEP

- If you plan on building rapport with a person who blogs, consider commenting below the blog – publicly, for double effect.

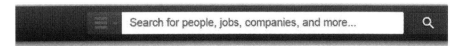

Inbox

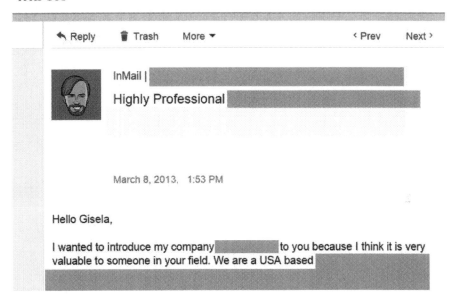

| ↩ Reply | 🗑 Trash | More ▼ | | ‹ Prev | Next › |

InMail |

Highly Professional

March 8, 2013. 1:53 PM

Hello Gisela,

I wanted to introduce my company to you because I think it is very valuable to someone in your field. We are a USA based

[Inevitably, reading e-mails out loud puts the spotlight on strange phrases like "someone in your field." – Someone? – And, which field?

While sometimes this type of phrase looks cool on the screen, reading such a dramatic phrase out loud reveals how it sounds to the recipient.]

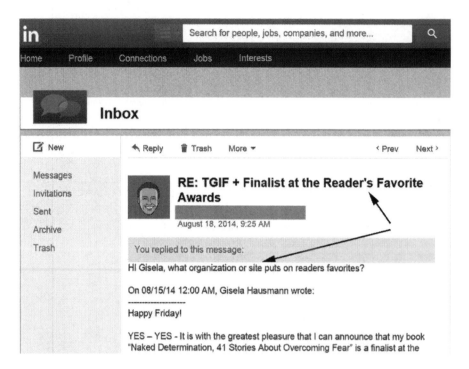

[*Simply googling "Readers Favorite Award" would have led the sender of this e-mail to the website www.readersfavorite.com.*]

ACTION STEP

- Before sending an e-mail with a request for information, always research the topic. The above listed e-mail seems to suggest that the sender is either lazy, does not know how to use Google, or does not value his recipient's time.

Lastly, I will stipulate that all of us can "feel" what the senders think when they write the e-mails we receive. This following e-mail also points at another problem, which, I am one hundred percent certain, happened unintentionally.

From:

To: "gisela.hausmann@

Sent: Wednesday, July 24, 2013 10:14 PM

Subject: Review of my

Hi Gisela,

As I mentioned on facebook, I just finished the final edit of my novel, I really appreciate your offer to review my book. I have attached it to this email. I plan on releasing it on October 23. If you can, can you please read it before then and have your review ready in time? If so, I will use a part from it for the blurb.

Thank you very much

Sincerely

Firstly, this e-mail is the sender's ME-mail, not an e-mail. It "screams" ME... ME... ME...

The main problem of ME-mails is that they put the emphasis on something that is well known but not really appreciated: Everybody wants something!

Of course, this has always been the case, but only one hundred years ago most people could not reach more than two hundred people; sending letters and making phone calls with the intent of "wanting something" was too expensive.

These days everybody can reach everybody. Consequently, lots of people send request e-mails. Since e-mail has been around for decades all of us have received thousands if not tens of thousands of ME-mails. Consequently, most of us have learned to ignore ME-mails.

If you want somebody else to do something, it is crucial that you write about "the something" and not about "I want...", "I need..."

More than 10% of this e-mail consists out of the words "I" and "my" (8/62 words).

Still, I want to use this particular e-mail to show how any e-mail can be improved. Here it is again:

From:

To: "gisela.hausmann@

Sent: Wednesday, July 24, 2013 10:14 PM

Subject: Review of my

Hi Gisela,

As I mentioned on facebook, I just finished the final edit of my novel, I really appreciate your offer to review my book. I have attached it to this email. I plan on releasing it on October 23. If you can, can you please read it before then and have your review ready in time? If so, I will use a part from it for the blurb.

Thank you very much

Sincerely

1) Eliminate sentence #1, "As I mentioned on facebook, I just finished the final edit of my novel..." It is redundant. Obviously, a writer had to finish his novel to present and publish it.

2) Add an always powerful "Thank you" and rephrase to write "Thank you for offering to read and review my novel ...xyz..."

3) Rephrase "I have attached" to "A .pdf copy is attached." Or "Please find a .pdf copy attached." (This eliminates one of the omnipresent "I's").

4) Rephrase "I plan on releasing..." to "The planned publication date is October 23."

5) Replace "If you can, can you please..." with "Should this timeframe be too short, could you please let me know?" It is always a good idea to ask a question. Savvy e-mail writers use questions to get written confirmations; for example, a possible reply would be "Thx. Three months are just fine." In the event the recipient replies with "Sorry. I am tied up for the next few months," the sender can always consider new steps, at that time.

6) Here is the unintended problem. The sentence "...and have your review ready in time? **If so, I will use** a part from it for the blurb..." clearly suggests that the sender of this e-mail expects to receive a positive review, even though the sender is aware that I, the recipient, have not seen, let alone read his book. He attached it to his e-mail.

   Authors know that such a suggestion is against Amazon's rules, even though the sender does not propose bribery or payment.

   Even readers who aren't authors and have never reviewed a book will sense that this suggestion may be against the rules. However, knowing the writer of this e-mail, I am sure that he did not mean to do anything improper but probably got carried away with excitement after finishing his novel. **Still, in a different industry, under different circumstances, words written in haste can cause huge problems.** You and I have read about law cases in which seemingly innocent e-mails were part of a problem.

Never, ever send an e-mail without re-reading it and **LISTENING** to your own words!

8) A better way to express the same wish would have been to write, "Obviously I really hope that you can read and review my novel in time; maybe I could even use one or two sentences of your review for my book's blurb."

9) Any request e-mail will be a more appealing e-mail if the sender writes, "If you have any questions please drop me a line or contact me at xxx-xxx-xxxx."

10) Improve "Thank you very much" by writing instead "Thank you again."

11) Delete "Sincerely". It is old-fashioned.

ACTION STEPS

- Check if you overuse the word "I" in your e-mails. An easy trick is to highlight every occurrence of the words "I", "my", and "me".
- Use questions to get a commitment from the recipient.

From: ▮▮▮▮▮▮

To: "gisela.hausmann@▮▮▮

Sent: Wednesday, July 24, 2013 10:14 PM

Subject: Review of my ▮▮▮▮

Hi Gisela,

As ▮ mentioned on facebook, ▮ just finished the final edit of ▮▮ novel. ▮▮▮▮▮ really appreciate your offer to review ▮▮ book. ▮ have attached it to this email. ▮ plan on releasing it on October 23. If you can, can you please read it before then and have your review ready in time? If so, ▮ will use a part from it for the blurb.

Thank you very much

Sincerely

▮▮▮▮▮▮

- You could also count the number of words of your e-mail and count the occurrences of the "me-me-me"-words and figure out the percentage of words that talk about "I" (the sender). Any number over 5% is too high.
- Soften the impact of the word "I" at the beginning of a sentence by adding adverbs and phrases like "In the meantime", "Obviously", "Naturally", "Of course". For instance, "Naturally, I hope...", "In the meantime I will..." etc.
- Think of creative ways to rephrase your sentence, to use the word "you" instead of "I". For instance, "Dear Joe, I want/need/request..." can be rephrased to "Dear Joe, Just to keep you in the loop: We will need..." (Using "we" always suggests team spirit.)

7 – THE ENDING SALUTATION & SIGNATURE

The ending salutation too is a terrific opportunity to shine and to distinguish your e-mail from most of the other e-mails in your business partner's Inbox.

As a general rule, never again use the ending salutation "sincerely" – never, ever! My daughter once quipped very brilliantly: "Is there anything less sincere than sincerely... I sincerely doubt it..."

"Sincerely" is the most overused word in all e-mails – worldwide. It was first recorded as a subscription to letters in 1702. Since then it has become overused and uncreative. Writing "sincerely" indicates "I am like everybody else" and/or "you are like everybody else to me." In the 21st century, we strive for distinguishing ourselves.

Picking the perfect ending salutation is important for two reasons. Firstly, it gives you the opportunity to make a great final impression. Don't waste it by saying something the recipient knows, like "thank you and good-bye". Instead, use the ending salutation to make your final mark on the conversation, to make the point and to show how much you care. The more details you mention, the more you prove that indeed you care. How else would you know all the specifics?

Examples:

- "Many, many thanks... What a great team effort this was. At this time I want to thank xyz for ....(list of all major accomplishments how the team excelled)"

  indicates that you are a born team leader. Your last thought before you wrap up is your team. This is an obvious managerial quality. Do not forget to copy all relevant department managers!

- "Hope that this first bit of information helps... I'll be in touch immediately once I know more. In the meantime please advise any findings on your part which may help to reach our common goal faster. As always..."

  indicates that though you may not have all information needed, you are working on it and you care.

- "TGIF!"

  indicates: "I know how you feel and maybe I feel the same way..." (Obviously, TGIF is not a perfect ending salutation for everybody, but at least I know quite few people who really appreciated reading this on a Friday starting at noon. The word builds solidarity in certain situations.)

All of these examples demonstrate personal engagement and additional effort to strengthen your various business relationships.

Secondly, choosing a perfect ending salutation can help to build your own brand. Brand building via e-mail requires that you always use the same ending salutation, like a slogan to 'sign out'. This ending salutation needs to fit to your personality and your industry.

Example: As a lawyer, you might not want to use the salutation "Godspeed" but rather "As always"; after all, hiring a lawyer means not leaving things in God's hands.

To find your ideal choice you may want to investigate one or a few of the dozens of websites, which list hundreds of salutations.

Some of my favorites are:

- "Thank you for your consideration"

- "Yours respectfully"

- "With kindest personal regards"

- "Godspeed"

- "Onward and Upward"

- "Deeply grateful"

- "Warmest greetings to all"

- "Cheers"

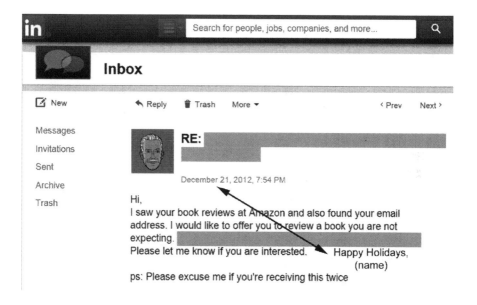

[Not focusing on the number of sentences that begin with the word "I", this e-mail can be improved quite easily by adding the recipient's name, plus a seasonal salutation like "Happy Holidays (name)." Sadly, the postscript indicates that this is a mass e-mail, which means this writer may have spent hours looking for and contacting book reviewers, which probably did

not result in many reviews.]

Inbox

↰ Reply   🗑 Trash   More ▾   Next ›

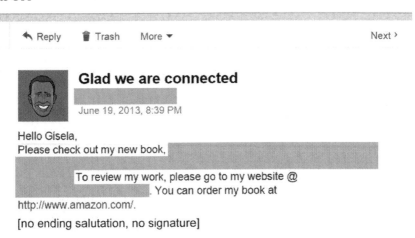

Glad we are connected

June 19, 2013, 8:39 PM

Hello Gisela,
Please check out my new book,

To review my work, please go to my website @
. You can order my book at
http://www.amazon.com/.
[no ending salutation, no signature]

[At social media platforms, we do not sign our messages because they are displayed next to our avatar. This has led to the bad habit of many people not signing their e-mails.

Writing best e-mails is all about "creating a personal connection." E-mails that aren't signed are NOT personal, obviously.

Especially when the sender wants the recipient to do something, a nice ending salutation as well as signing the request could have a positive effect.]

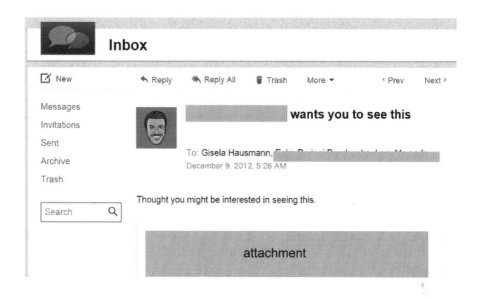

[Is there anybody who appreciates receiving and reading this type of e-mail? Without greeting and ending salutation?

It is also quite obvious that this e-mail is a mass e-mail. Either the sender forgot to uncheck Linkedin's e-mail option "Allow recipients to see each other's e-mail addresses" or he did not care.

This example illustrates another important topic. If obviously it is important to write best e-mails to individual people, it is even more important to write best e-mails if the same e-mail is meant to reach many people.

This e-mail has no personal appeal at all. It had fifty names in copy (cc'd).]

ACTION STEP

- Always sign with your name, even though your e-mail signature includes your name. Typing your name under your e-mail is more personal; it shows interest and caring. Trying to build a great business relationship most certainly warrants the little effort of typing your own name!

- Additionally, design a great signature. Your signature is your digital business card and therefore needs to be a matter of pride. Take advantage of all features your e-mail program offers.

SUGGESTIONS FOR IMPROVEMENTS OF COMMON PHRASES

The most effective e-mails with personal appeal are e-mails that are

a) truly personal,
b) appreciating the recipient's efforts,
c) focused and concise to avoid wasting the recipient's time

Like with every skill, practice makes one perfect. Start by going over each first draft and improve every single sentence. At the same time, delete redundant sentences.

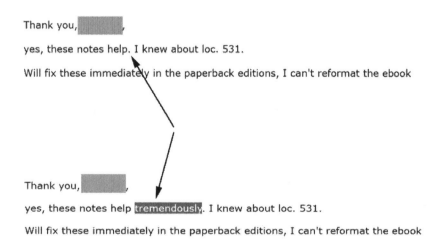

Thank you,

yes, these notes help. I knew about loc. 531.

Will fix these immediately in the paperback editions, I can't reformat the ebook

Thank you,

yes, these notes help tremendously. I knew about loc. 531.

Will fix these immediately in the paperback editions, I can't reformat the ebook

Especially if you want the recipient to do something for you, try to see things from his perspective.

***

The "cold-call" e-mail introduction:

(-) Hi, Gisela, I'm …xyz…, author and …

(-) Hi Gisela, I wanted to introduce my company …xyz…

(+) Hello Gisela, It appears we have a common love – books! Excited to meet you…"

***

The follow-up connection e-mail:

(-) "… I am glad we are connected…"

(-) "… Thank you so much for the opportunity to connect! …"

(+) "… Thank you for befriending me (accepting my request to connect) **right away (so quickly)**…"

[Always write "quickly," even if it took a few days until the other party accepted the friend request. All that means is that other party was busy.]

***

The "things aren't going well e-mail"

(-) "… Hi Gisela, well, I wish things were going a lot better. Sales have been slower than anticipated…"

(+) "… Hello Gisela, Thank you so much for … xyz… I was excited to find your e-mail. I am still working on ways to improve my book sales and am hoping that you …"

***

The acknowledgement e-mail:

(-) "… Thank you, I will take a look! …"

(-) "… THX. I will check out …"

[Nobody cares what anybody WILL DO in the future. The best way is to respond AFTER you have read/studied the information. If you don't intend to read the information, just don't say anything. Nobody expects everybody to read every bit of information he sends. These days we offer information. Our business partners decide what they want to read. Therefore, keep everything interesting, including acknowledgement e-mails.]

(+) "... Dear Gisela, OMG ! Now I have to thank you, not only for your time but also for your..."
(+) "... Fabulous, Gisela. That's what I wanted to hear – a contrary argument to set me straight..."

***

The "thank-you"- e-mail:

(-) Thanks for this info. Best wishes:-)
(-) Great Gisela! Thank you! (name)

These two "thank-you" e-mails are the equivalent of a "like" in the world of social media. "Liking" alone won't lead to a prosperous connection. To make an impression, we have to be SPECIFIC & PERSONAL! Any thank-you e-mail will only have a positive effect if it's clear that it comes from the heart!

(+) "... Dear (name), Though I posted below your absolutely awesome review, I wanted to thank you again, "personally", without the "public watching"..."

(+) "Love it, (name), THANK YOU! Love the humor in your review..."

***

The Christmas e-mail:

(-) "... Hi, I've sent you a Season's Greetings eCard. Click here to view…"

[No personal greeting, no personalization, but instead a mass e-mail with a link. Please compare with]

(+) "Thank you Gisela, Merry Christmas... Really miss talking with you! Hope you…"

7 WORDS YOU SHOULD NEVER USE IN AN E-MAIL

***

" I "

[A professional e-mail is neither a diary nor an autobiography. It has a purpose – to introduce a product or service, to make an offer, to ask for clarification, to apply for a job, or similar professional goals. Therefore, the e-mail should describe the product and explain how and why it is important to the recipient (you) and not why it is important to the person who wrote the e-mail (I). Use the word 'I' as sparingly as possible.]

***

"LET ME INTRODUCE MYSELF…" (at the beginning of the e-mail)

[Nooo, don't introduce yourself, introduce the product; unless you are writing an e-mail at a dating website and you are the product.]

***

"NO PROBLEM"

[Replying "no problem" means losing an opportunity. Typically, the sender of the original e-mail informed a recipient that something isn't possible; for instance, the sender cannot meet a deadline or cannot attend a meeting. By replying with "no problem", the recipient is saying that he does not care or that the original sender's contribution or attendance is not important, urgent, or relevant.

A much better way to respond is to write, "Dear (name), Thank you for informing me of … (this or that)… Considering the situation, I truly appreciate that you'll make an effort to… (do this or that)… until… (mention the new deadline)… Should any other issues arise, please let me know right away. Maybe I can help. With many thanks, (name)]

***

"RECEIVE YOUR GIFT…"

[Never use the word 'gift' unless you are representing a charitable organization.
Most of us know that only charitable organizations give 'real' gifts.
If you want to boost sales, offer a price reduction or a special deal instead. Offering a gift implies, "If you buy anything from me I can recover my costs for producing the gift. Plus, I am also going to charge you for the gifts of all the people who did not become my customers."
Everything costs something and most people want to be reimbursed. Even writing newsletters costs something – time, which can be charged.]

***

"BUT"

[Writing "but" means nullifying everything that was said before. E.g. "I liked it, but…" In plain translation, this means "I did not like it enough." The sour taste prevails. In a short e-mail you have to make every word count. Therefore, never nullify the impact of any of your words. A much better and more encouraging way to present the same message is, "I liked … (this and that)… a lot/tremendously. (Mention 2-3 details.)

Maybe, changing the ... (element you did not like) ... to ... (whatever you think needs to be done)... would increase the impact even more? What do you think?"]

***

"ALWAYS" and "NEVER"

[If the last fifteen years have taught us anything, it is that things aren't the way they 'always' used to be anymore and things which we thought would 'never' be possible have become part of our daily lives. Using 'always' and 'never' makes writers/senders look rigid and out of tune with reality. Also, if you uttered either one in an e-mail to a mean boss, these words almost beg the recipient to think, "We'll see about that."]

***

"SECRET"

[Is there anybody who wants to do business with somebody who divulges secret information? Everybody knows that sharing secrets demonstrates character flaws. Additionally, once something is out on the market, it isn't a secret any longer. A more attractive way to describe such knowledge is the term "previously unpublished".]

***

TYPOS, MISSPELLINGS, & THE MOST INFAMOUS WRITING ERROR

Since I am an author, I spend lot of time with other authors, publishers, and book reviewers. In these circles, people talk a lot about typos and how terrible typos and misspellings are. Many of my friends in the publishing industry think that anybody who makes typos and misspellings cannot be taken seriously. My experience is different; I have worked with many competent people who have made typos and misspellings. While typos and misspelling should be avoided, I think the MESSAGE is far more important. Then again, there are limits as illustrated in the following example:

***

Dear Gisela,
Thank you for ur reply.
Ur idea sounds really good, I will think of making some more market research and convert my dissertation into an ebook...that would be very beneficial for my person...my name would be more recognisable ;)
Anyway, I reckon u r a very busy person...but if you want, I could send you a set of questions I am addressing to various individuals about their reading experiences and views on print/ebook. It's ten questions which need descriptive answering ;)
Anyway, if you don't want to get involved, that is absolutely fine :)
I appreciate ur help already :)
Thanks a lot for everything.
Let me know what do you think of that.
Looking forward to hearing from you.
Best wishes,
(name)

[Yes, I too wondered which college this student attends.]

***

Finally, there the three words which I most often see being used incorrectly:

- Your
- You're
- You are

Since these words are basic and they are taught in elementary school, using them incorrectly is worse than mixing up 'adverse and averse' or 'criteria and criterion'.

Instead of writing "You're welcome", you could proclaim "It's been my pleasure". Spell check will correct any misspellings in this phrase, whereas it won't correct "your" or "you're" when either one is applied incorrectly.

EXCEPTION: Never misspell a recipient's name. Misspelling somebody's name indicates that you don't care about this person.

THE THANK-YOU E-MAIL & THE SEASONAL SURPRISE E-MAIL

Between 5% and 10% of your e-mails should be "THANK-YOU" e-mails. If you cannot find a reason to send at least one thank-you e-mail per day, you are either working with the wrong people or for the wrong company. Most people work extremely hard and receive little thanks. Being the person who thanks them elevates you to becoming that special person whose e-mails everybody wants to open and read. Additionally, doing so demonstrates your leadership qualities.

Thank-you e-mails make everybody happy, the praised colleague, the boss, and you yourself. When eventually you will be promoted, the people whose talents and capabilities you have pointed out over the years will be happy to work for you.

Be sure to mention the specific qualities your colleagues brought to the table. Leaders need to demonstrate the ability to recognize individual strengths so they can effectively combine them for success. By mentioning your colleagues' talents in your e-mails, you prove that you could be their leader.

Your colleagues and business partners will also appreciate the SEASONAL SURPRISE E-MAIL. Obviously, the various holidays are a great opportunity to relax a bit and have fun while also strengthening your contacts. Then again, how many Eastern bunnies, Thanksgiving cornucopias, and Santas can and do we appreciate? A carefully selected and tasteful joke, fitting to the season, can help build your brand as a witty, intelligent business partner with a human side. Be careful to avoid corny jokes and you will achieve great results!

WHAT ABOUT IF ALL OF THIS DOES NOT WORK?

You have to try again! It is well known that on a bad day many people simply delete all e-mails they do not expect. Though you may have crafted a perfect e-mail, the recipient may have never opened it. Unfortunately, at times, all of us are overburdened and things like that can happen.

A BRIEF REMINDER

E-mails are legal documents and having to provide e-mail records is a standard procedure of full disclosure in legal cases. It implies that, sometimes, an e-mail that you wrote in haste might be read in court in the future, even if you never did anything wrong. Additionally, e-mail accounts sometimes get hacked. On the off chance that this happens to your company, you always want to make sure that your e-mail is the one that sounds best.

Please note: Considering the fight against terrorism, the laws may be broadened and may also include information stored in clouds.

27 EXAMPLES OF LUDICROUS E-MAILS

All of these are real e-mails that I have received. Annotations and thoughts are noted in brackets […] underneath.

TOO SHORT, UNPROFESSIONAL E-MAILS

***

"Thanks honey,…"

[No, it is not cute.]

***

"That is fine."
(organization's signature block but no sender's name)

[No greeting, no name… In other words, it's NOT fine.]

***

"Hi,
I saw your reviews and had the chance to find your e-mail address. I would like to offer you to review a book you are not expecting. It's called "…xyz…."
Let me know if you are interested.
ps please excuse me if your receiving this twice"

[1) I…I…I … So, I gather this e-mail is about you. 2) No, indeed, I was not expecting this 3) 'Let me know', but no signature? Why would I? I don't even know who you are! 4) 'receiving this twice' = a dead giveaway that this utterance is part of a mass e-mail 5) BTW, what's the book/product about? and 'your' instead of 'you're' misspelled by a writer or a publisher??]

"Hello,
Would you be interested in reviewing the …xyz-Kit?
If so please send me you address and i will get it rite over to you
Thanks!"

[It is hard to believe that this e-mail comes from a marketing person of any US company.]

***

Hello,
I am the marketing manager of …ABC…
I have noticed that you are pretty good at writing reviews on amazon.
And it seems you have plenty of fans love your reviews.
I am glad to offer you our fantastic …xyz… for your wonderful review on Amazon.
Please reply with your shipping address if you are willing to receive and review it.

By the way, recommend our …uvw… to you,
It suits to …uvw….
Thanks and Best Regards.
(name)/Marketing Manager.
… a US company…

[Again, it is hard to believe that this e-mail comes from a marketing person of any US company.]

***

Yourr scanned documents cannot be printed. Fax them to me at xxx-xxx-xxxx

*[No greeting, typo in the first word, and commanding tone…
from the secretary of a lawyer's office. It must be really hard to find good help.]*

***

BS E-MAILS

[BS e-mails are e-mails that don't say anything; they have no real message.]

***

"Thank you, and the same to you." (no greeting, no signature)

[That's all?]

***

Thanks for sharing this, Gisela. Really interesting stuff! (no greeting, no signature)

[Platitude]

***

Thank you Gisela for your involved concern. I will follow your advice. And of course seek further advice

[No greeting, no signature, and what exactly are you trying to say?]

***

"… between them have published over 140 books, sold more than 50,000 copies, hit the Amazon bestseller list more than a dozen times and earned six-figures in royalties (including as much as $13,000 in a single month)…"

[Yes, numbers are important, but they have to add up! 50,000 divided by 140 equals 357 copies per title, that's hardly impressive. While I don't want to question these numbers, they need to be presented in a meaningful way.]

***

Your valuable comments are most welcome…trust me, it matters a lot to me.
Warm personal Regards,

[No greeting, no signature. Is there a message in this array of catch phrases?]

As we approach the 228th anniversary of Declaration of Independence in USA we ask all concerned citizens to consider this Declaration of XYZ as a (whatever).
And a four figure matching contribution continues the effort. Perhaps one of You are acquainted with a (whatever) Investor to whom a qualified executive briefing for this campaign can be attractive.
(name)

[? ? ? (Although it's is hard to believe, the writer is an American.)]

I like your presentation— book wise that is—and wonder if you might be interested in some exposure in terms of expanding your audience. I have some design and editorial issues re upcoming projects (book and film). If you're interested you my e-mail xyz@xyz.com

[Incoherent platitudes. Is the sender trying to sell me his services or does he want to me to solve his issues?]

Hey Gisela,
Really appreciate you becoming part of my growing network of positive influencers. I like to spend a few minutes getting to know more about the people that choose to become my

network. I would love to find out if there are any ways I can help support your life dreams, either now or in the future. When works to schedule a quick introductory call?

Have a lovely Sunday,
(no signature)

[a) Don't call me "hey" plus b) I doubt that anybody who doesn't know that 'hey' is not an appropriate greeting can support my life dreams, either now or in the future.]

***

Hi Gisela ,

If you registered for the webinar, you were sent a replay, if you did not get it i would be happy to forward this to you at whatever address you like, thanks

(name)

[It appears this webinar does not have a title or topic. And, no, I did not register for it.]

***

CRAZY E-MAILS

***

Thanks babe x (no greeting, no sig)

[?]

***

Thank you for your prompt reply.
Could you send me e-mail addresses of Oprah Winfrey or
some other internationally acclaimed philanthropist or
evangelists.

*[No greeting, no signature, plus I wonder if personal friends of
Oprah or 'some other internationally acclaimed philanthropist
or evangelist' would reply to this e-mail.]*

***

I like your style
DON'T MISS: xyz
2015 xyz PR & Marketing Kit: All New

*[No greeting, no signature. I don't think I am going to hire this
person to run a marketing campaign.]*

***

TOO MUCH OR TOO LITTLE INFORMATION E-MAILS

***

(No greeting)
I just realized I mistyped your e-mail address on the instructions I just sent.
Hope you have a great week.
(no signature, but a religious quote in lieu of a signature)

[Sent by a paralegal. (She no longer works at that office.)]

***

(no greeting)
The power of coaching and self-coaching. 2015 is ours! Let's ROCK! In this blog post (almost 4K words, I spent the whole morning writing it for you) I share my best strategies, steps for success and fulfillment as well as the best health, wealth, business and happiness coaching resources. Enjoy! (no signature)

[Who has time to read a 4K blog? Does anybody really believe you wrote it in one morning? And, if you did write 4K words in one morning, can this blog be good? Professional writers need longer to write 4K words.]

***

Considering your success with books as well as your publishing background, I was looking to see if you would be interested in publishing these two great children's books which I have written. I have been wanting to publish these books for a long time.
Regards, (signature)

[No greeting, no info – What makes 'these books' great? Plus, sorry to break your bubble, but all of us want something.]

***

Hi Gisela,
Thank you for the connection...we are in the development process of a feature film here in the NE US area and are looking for funding. If you or someone you know may be interested in hearing more please let me know.
beautiful name by the way!
(signature)

[48 words – absolutely no effort! What kind of feature film? Low-budget? Sci-fi? The difference could be in the millions of dollars. Also, do you always ask people who you don't know too well for money?]

***

I prefer the words of Gen. Rommel who stated in the absence of orders find something and kill it
(no greeting, no signature)

[? I wonder if e-mails like this need to be reported somewhere!]

***

okey dokey, coming your way, but expect a delay as I am between shipments
right now.
thx many times Gisela.
(Initials)

[No greeting, plus the writer never shipped the book, which did not really come as a surprise after reading that e-mail.]

***

Hi Gisela,

I like your article – could you please get me into these fields in Amazon. My book is with them but nothing is happening. Thanks.
(no signature)

[Do you know anything about publishing and – writing?]

***

Hello,
We are promoting XYZ book from Amazon
All earned money go to … abc organization...
Please give us 5 stars on Amazon!
Thanks,
(signature, description of book included but omitted to protect the sender's information)

[If a middle school student had written this e-mail, it would have been really sweet. Sadly, the writer is quite a bit older.]

***

GLOBAL IMPACT

All of us like to think that we live in a global society; and, we do!

What does this mean with regards to e-mail?

To Gisela Hausmann

Hi Gisela,

First of all thanks for considering me to review your book and many congratulations for the success of your ebook " " and hope it will cross many other milestones.

I have accepted your gift of ebook on Amazon and I am committed to provide a genuine review of your book by date

Wishing you all the best and I will email you again after reviewing your book on Amazon.

Thank you

This authentic, original e-mail was written by a foreign book reviewer. It is as perfect as any e-mail could be. The writer

1) thanks me for considering him
2) expresses positive feelings about our business relationship
3) confirms that he will do what I invited him to do
4) confirms that he will follow Amazon's rules by providing a "genuine" review
5) provides a timeline
6) offers a thoughtful ending salutation

and, he does all of that in 83 words.

Writing best e-mail matters – worldwide.

HOW DO YOU KNOW IF YOUR BUSINESS PARTNERS APPRECIATE YOUR E-MAILS?

There is a direct correlation between "appreciating you and your e-mails" and the time frame until you'll receive a reply.

All of us are in charge of our own Inbox; we decide which e-mails we open right away, which ones we put off, and which ones we delete without ever looking at them.

Therefore, the faster you receive a reply the more appreciated you and your e-mails are.

Not to brag but to point out this sender's e-mail writing skills, I am including an e-mail, whose writer delivered the ultimate compliment for me: "We'll miss your e-mails."

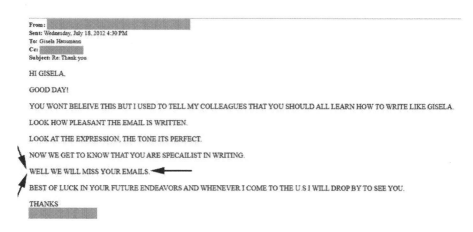

From:
Sent: Wednesday, July 18, 2012 4:30 PM
To: Gisela Hausmann
Cc:
Subject: Re: Thank you

HI GISELA,

GOOD DAY!

YOU WONT BELEIVE THIS BUT I USED TO TELL MY COLLEAGUES THAT YOU SHOULD ALL LEARN HOW TO WRITE LIKE GISELA.

LOOK HOW PLEASANT THE EMAIL IS WRITTEN.

LOOK AT THE EXPRESSION, THE TONE ITS PERFECT.

NOW WE GET TO KNOW THAT YOU ARE SPECAILIST IN WRITING.

WELL WE WILL MISS YOUR EMAILS.

BEST OF LUCK IN YOUR FUTURE ENDEAVORS AND WHENEVER I COME TO THE U.S I WILL DROP BY TO SEE YOU.

THANKS

This e-mail writer made me blush.

How often does one get to hear that one's e-mails will be missed?

It is my hope that this book will help you to write e-mails your business partners will look forward to receiving, even on the day before they go on vacation.

It is also my hope that this book will help you to enjoy writing e-mails as much as I do. Of the many skills people work on getting better every day, writing best e-mail is one that will pay back for a lifetime.

Write Your E-mails Like a Soldier in the Field

Imagine yourself being a soldier in Vietnam, long before cell phones, social media, and video chat were invented. The only way you would have been able to communicate with family and friends was via snail mail.

Replies meant that your base cared about you, that you were still "in the game" even if it had been months since you saw your people last. Of course your family would never forget you, but what about your girlfriend? Was maybe another guy trying to score with her and promising her bigger and better things? And, what about your buddies from school? Were they pushing their careers and maybe forgetting about you?

Considering that there was not going to be an opportunity for a face-to-face meeting anytime soon, you'd weigh each word carefully. You'd brag a bit about heroic acts while at the same time you'd assure everybody that you were with a great team, that you had the very best support in case things got tight. You would write about your platoon and describe how they contributed. Also, knowing that each letter might be your last one, you'd make certain that you wrote how much you thought and cared about your loved ones.

Most certainly, you'd never write platitudes, because every single word was part of shaping the life you would enjoy – if you made it out of the jungle.

In 2003, Donald Trump told Mark Burnett, the producer of "Survivor," to forget "his Amazons and Africas"; in Trump's opinion New York was the real jungle. Together they went on to produce "The Apprentice."
The show's candidates wrote "letters" too, only these were e-mails. They too weighed every word carefully; surely none of

them wanted to get caught forgetting to put something important in writing.

There are many more similarities between the war in this jungle and in that jungle. Not surprisingly, "The Art of War" by Sun Tzu has become a cult book for business leaders.

Everybody has to succeed with his own mission and not worry about some distant front. Today's business e-mails are as important as the US troops' letters to their loved ones and friends; they are the building blocks for our future in business. Therefore,

1) Never send a canned e-mail. They hardly ever lead to exceptional success, just like military awards and decorations aren't given for doing "canned actions."

2) Mention your team, often. Nobody believes that a "lone wolf" can be successful forever.

3) Write often to stay in touch. Everybody likes to read a friendly e-mail for no reason, instead of only being asked for "care packages."

4) Make each word count! When writing important e-mails apply Steve Job's concept of wondering if he was doing what he would do if he knew it was the last day of his life. Similarly, write each business e-mail as if this was your last chance to pull a major business deal ashore. This will lead to success.

5) Be personal! Just like the letters written during the Vietnam War, your e-mails are the lifeline to your future. The result of each e-mail should be furthering a relationship that will last a long time.

***

Do You Want to Sell Something or Get Somebody to Do Something?

Most of us send e-mails trying to convince somebody to do business with us. Every day, 100 billion e-mails get sent, worldwide. That implies that our e-mails have to be effective and PERSONAL.

Not only do we, the senders, have to prove that

1. we and our products are special,
2. we also have to prove that the recipient is special and important to us, and not just "another" client.

Having analyzed 100,000+ e-mails in the past I can say with certainty – It's all about the little details.

Here is an illustration from another arena – social media.

Last week I posted that my cat Artemis got sick. That prompted 87 of my 475 friends to send well wishes to Artemis. Quite a few wished HIM a speedy recovery even though the posting announced that SHE is not well. A few friends renamed her ARTEMUS or ARTIMUS. These wishes were sort of bunched together. Naturally, I know how this happened. Somebody saw the picture of my sick cat and barely registered the name...

Artemis... Artimus... something like that... **E or I... I or U...**

The first person to (not really) read the posting and then write "Artimus" assumed that my cat is a boy cat. Some people, who sent their well wishes later, skipped reading the posting and read the last few comments which caused them to think that my cat is a male cat.

Naturally, Artemis does not care how her name is spelled.

Plus, since she is neutered, she probably does not care if she is a he or a she.

Here is the **SIGNIFICANCE** of this story.

Of course, I (and everybody else who read the entire posting) could identify who did NOT read it. However, even for me, **IT IS IMPOSSIBLE to know** who of my almost 500 FB friends

- cares enough about me to know that I have a female cat named Artemis or
- who simply **read only this one specific posting with UTMOST CARE, maybe even jotted down notes, and then composed a thoughtful reply**.

It is the same for business e-mails. When we receive a thoughtful e-mail, which addresses our needs, we do not know if the sender has known about us or our business for years or if the sender has acquired his knowledge in the last three hours. And, in reality it does not matter. This person will probably be the best business partner. His or her e-mail advertises "I am a business partner, who works hard; I care about every detail, AND therefore I will do the best job for YOU."

Thus, MAKE THAT EFFORT! **The people who get the business are always the people who write every e-mail as if it will be the last e-mail they'll ever write.**

***

8 Reasons Why You Should Love E-mail & 7 Ways to Make Yours More Effective

- E-mail is the most effective way to reach customers, acquire new customers, and sell to customers – worldwide.

- A 2014 study by McKinsey & Company proved that e-mail marketing is nearly 40 times as effective as Facebook and Twitter combined.

- 91% of all US customers use e-mail, whereas only 71% of online adults use Facebook, 23% of online adults use Twitter, and 28% use LinkedIn. (2014).

- Additionally, the average order value as a result of e-mail marketing is 17% higher than that of social media marketing, which may be contributed to the fact that e-mail is more personal than social media.

- Obviously, customers who receive e-mail offers believe that they belong to a selected group that has the opportunity to take advantage of a special offer.

Advantages of writing e-mails, particularly for the Small Business Owner

- Writing e-mails levels the playing field. A skillfully written e-mail from a small business owner can look superior to a lackluster e-mail written by an employee from a huge corporation.

- Quite often, small business owners receive unexpected or unusual requests, to which they may not have all answers; in fact, they may not even know if they can fulfill the request. Sending a skillfully written e-mail buys them time to solve their issues while looking professional.

- Writing great pitching e-mails to media persons gives small business owners the opportunity to get exposure via guest blogging or to be featured on TV or in a magazine.

So, what can you do to write most effective e-mails with personal appeal?

1) When getting ready to compose an e-mail, think "product – product – product" and focus solely on how your product or service will affect your customers' needs.

2) Avoid writing the word "I" as much as possible, instead – find ways to say "you" and "your".

3) Avoid writing standard phrases. Instead of using run-of-the-mill phrases like "Please feel free to call me" write "If you have any additional questions, please call me – anytime."

4) Never ever use a template. If you found it on Google, chances are somebody else is using the same template. If writing is not your strong suit rather hire a writer to create unique content.

5) Never ever use a standard greeting like "hi" and "sincerely". "Sincerely" is the most overused word in all e-mails – worldwide. Writing "sincerely" indicates "I am like everybody else" and/or "you are like everybody else to me." In the 21st century, we strive for distinguishing ourselves.

6) Avoid simply "listing" features of your products or services. Ideally, your e-mail should have the same personal impact like a short meeting with a future client.

7) Read your e-mails out loud to yourself before you click that "send"- button. Listening to your own writing is the easiest way to find out how your e-mail will sound to the recipient. Don't believe that this works? – Just open your sent-folder and read any e-mail you sent four weeks ago! Does it sound effective and personal?

***

Why HR Needs to Test Job Applicants for their Email Writing Skills

As the author of the blog, "Know your next president's email writing skills (not only Hillary's) – a blog series" I have visited a few presidential campaign events in my area.

At one of these occasions I exchanged thoughts with one of the candidates' regional campaign director. I told him that his and the overall campaign director's emails were not effective – they listed their own names instead of their candidate's name as the senders.

"Your campaign should be about creating your candidate's brand," I said. "Even though you might not like to hear that – voters do not need to know your name because they can't vote for you. The way you have set up your campaign emails probably half of your emails get deleted, because people delete emails from people they don't know."

"Well, **I am a bit old-fashioned,**" he said. "I prefer talking on the phone."

"That's nice," I replied, "but history proves that you need to pay attention to these things. In 2007/08, then-candidate Barack Obama raised half-a-billion dollars with his email campaign. If done effectively, email campaigns yield great results."

"Oh – Wow – I better tell my campaign director."

To this day, not much has changed. The campaign manager added the name of his candidate at the end of his address. Subscribers can only see the candidate's name if they hover with their mouse over the sender's handle. (How many people do that?)

Also, the candidate isn't doing too well in the polls. "Well," you might think, "Students... enthusiastic fans... they are still kind of young... They don't know how this is done right."

Sadly, the problem is far more widespread.

Even though a 2014 study by McKinsey & Company proved that **email marketing is nearly 40 times as effective as Facebook and Twitter combined** and marketers themselves continue to rate email the most effective marketing strategy, human resources departments continue to administer personality tests instead of email writing tests.

Writing best emails is also not taught in US high schools and at most US colleges. The effect is mind boggling.

Here are a few of the hundreds of inadvertently funny or embarrassing emails I have received.

***

Re: [Event Replay]

Hi Gisela,

That was AMAZING! **We're** you there? If so, I hope ...

[*Even though the correct usage of "were", "we're", "we are" is taught in elementary school these three words are still among the most common incorrectly used words.*]

***

"Hello,

Would you be interested in reviewing the ...xyz-Kit?

If so please send me you address and i will get it rite over to you

Thanks!"

(Marketing Dept./ a US company)

[?]

***

(No greeting)

I just realized I mistyped your email address on the instructions I just sent.

Hope you have a great week.

(no signature, but a religious quote in lieu of a signature)

[Sent by a paralegal.]

***

Hello,

I am the marketing manager of ...(company)...

I have noticed that you are pretty good at writing reviews on amazon.

And it seems you have plenty of fans love your reviews.

I am glad to offer you our fantastic ...(product)... for your wonderful review on Amazon.

Please reply with your shipping address if you are willing to receive and review it.

By the way, recommend our ...(different product)... to you,

It suits to ...

Thanks and Best Regards.

(name)/Marketing Manager.

[... a US company...]

***

Yourr scanned documents cannot be printed. Fax them to me at xxx-xxx-xxxx

[sent by the secretary of a lawyer.]

95

These kinds of emails can destroy a budding business before it could even take off. They also **do damage** to an established business and even to a business which doesn't sell goods but offers services (e.g. a lawyer's office) because inevitably the recipient must wonder about the quality of services he/she will receive.

Writing best emails is a skill that needs to be taught, and human resources departments should test job applicants for their skills.

***

TWEETS from the #EmailEvangelist

These are some of my #EmailEvangelist tweets. Find the ones that speak to you and blast them out into the twitter universe. All of these tweets have less than 110 characters. If you add #EmailEvangelist I'll tweet right back.

*

*It's not an Inbox problem;
it's an email problem.*

*

You must write the email you wish others will read.

*

*Struggle not to write a bestseller but rather an email
that matters.
Success will follow by itself.*

*

*Until you have lost an email, you never realize
what value it represents,
having it in black and white.*

*

*I didn't attend the meeting, but I sent a nice email
saying I approved of it.*

*

To find out your real opinion of someone,
judge the impression you have
when you first see an email from them.

*

Your knowledge writes the email.
Your brains signal 'send'.

*

To me, some emails read like somebody
wrote a love letter to himself.

*

They call it email, because me-mail was too long.

*

Many emails are like the shock
produced by a freezing cold bath.

*

You're always too successful,
to read every email in your Inbox.

*

There's only one email strategy: Be concise!

'Classic.'
An email which people talk about in staff meetings
and don't read.

✱

I would have answered your email sooner,
but you sent too many too long ones.

✱

Email 101 is about choices:
It can't be all happiness to all people.

✱

A template for everybody is an email to nobody.

✱

Emails speak louder than phone calls.

✱

While I write this email, I have a pistol in one hand
and a sword in the other.

✱

This is not an email but my thoughts focusing on
what you need,
for a brief moment.

Emails have no limitations,
except the ones you don't write.

*

The present email is a very long one,
simply because I had no leisure to make it shorter.

*

This is not an email but my thoughts wrapped
around you
for a brief moment.

*

Don't count the emails, make the email count.

~*~

Gisela Hausmann's business philosophy about "naked (meaning no-fluff) books"

While I don't know how you learned about my book, my work is not just this book, it is of a whole series of books featuring only "naked (no-fluff) information."

Today, thousands of books get published every day; many of them feature a lot of fluff. I know that you don't have time to "work" your way through this fluff, because neither do I.

This is my books' concept:

1) **"Naked" how-to books** deliver knowledge in the shortest, most **efficient** and most entertaining manner; they are supported by **illustrations**, which show and tell.

2) "Naked" no-fluff books **energize readers**, because readers do not have to labor through the pages, but can see what works and why it works.

3) "Naked" books **empower readers** because reading no-fluff books builds up energy. Readers do not feel drained but feel energized from learning dozens of easy-to-follow strategies and solutions in a short time.

4) "Naked" is to books what **"lean"** is to business; waste information is removed, solutions and action steps are introduced.

5) "Naked" no-fluff books are **so 21st century**... Today, we do not have time to dig for solutions; we want to buy, learn, and win!

Please find more of my books at:

http://www.giselahausmann.com/books.html

To be informed when I release a new "naked (no-fluff) book," please subscribe here. As an email evangelist, I do not inundate people with a constant stream of emails; it does not work.

Soon to be released:

"Naked Truths About Getting Product Reviews on Amazon.com: 7 Insider tips to boost Sales"

http://www.giselahausmann.com/free-creative-ideas.html

BONUS CHECK LIST:

This is only a check-list. To see actual examples of how to improve each of the seven parts of an e-mail, please re-read the fitting chapter. Keep this check-list handy until you know it by heart.

*

#1 – The sender's (your) name

Adopt the mindset of the Vietnam War soldier I wrote about in my blog!

DON'T EVER THINK:

- "Let me see what shells out!"

THINK:

- "This may be the most important e-mail I write today!"
- "Many people write boring emails. This is *my* chance to stand out!"
- "Whatever I write will be associated with my name!"

***

#2 – The best time to send an e-mail

Always acknowledge the receipt of every important e-mail. That does not mean that you have to provide all answers, just acknowledge the receipt and indicate *when* you'll have all information.

If you want to add drama, send your e-mail late in the day or early in the morning. In the event that you aren't a morning person, you can compose your e-mail the day before and send it early the next day.

Please note: All e-mails have a "time stamp" (day/min/sec) from the minute/second you actually created it. If you compose your e-mail on the day before you send it, you need to open the e-mail and make any change like putting a space behind your name. This action will change the "time stamp" to the time you actually send your e-mail.

***

#3 – The attractive & effective subject line

Include a "number" or a "special character" in your subject line!

I won the 2016 Sparky Award "Best Subject Line," awarded by SparkPost, whose clients include Oracle, PayPal, Linkedin, Comcast, Twitter and more extremely reputable companies.

My winning contribution was that I could prove that even famous influencers open e-mails from people they don't know if the subject line features a "number" or a "special character." They are attention getters. Generally, people open (and respond) within half an hour of receiving the e-mail.

***

#4 – The greeting

DON'T WRITE:

"Hi." It is boring.

WRITE:

Any professional greeting that will get your recipient's attention like "Hello" or "Good morning."

Also, consult your calendar! People like to be reminded of holidays. If appropriate – Be creative! Writing:

> "Happy Groundhog Day, Charlie! Regarding that report (name of report) you wanted on your desk by Friday..."

is much more appealing than:

> "Hi, Charlie! Regarding that report (name of report) you wanted on your desk by Friday..."

***

#5 – The spelling of the recipient's name

Check for spelling errors – every time!

***

6 – The body of your e-mail

Read every important e-mail, at least three times!

Read every important e-mail out loud, at least once! (with a muffled voice)

Instead of thinking "I want to sell you ... convince you ... inform you... " think "What are YOUR (the recipient's) needs?"

This process gets easier if you make a conscious effort to replace as many "I's" as possible with "you's" or "we's."

*

DON'T WRITE:

"I saw that you were interested in... "

WRITE:

"*You* showed an interest in... *We* can help with..."

*

DON'T WRITE:

"I would like to introduce my ..."

WRITE:

"Just briefly: *We* specialize in... and *we* can help with... If *we* can assist in any way please send us an e-mail or call xxx-xxx-xxxx."

*

DON'T WRITE:

"I want to add you to my... "

WRITE:

"*You* and I have a common interest – (field of interest). Hope *you* will connect with me ..."

***

THANK-YOU E-MAIL

Write at least one thank-you e-mail – every single day! They add up and you'll become that much liked and appreciated person whose e-mails everybody wants to open first.

7 – The ending salutation & signature

Consider the ending salutation your last chance to make a favorable and memorable impression. Never ever write "sincerely." It is outdated (for at least a decade).

Maybe, you can make your ending salutation part of your brand. Hundreds of corporations spend millions, if not billions, of dollars to remind consumers what their brand is about.

Every e-mail gives you the opportunity to do the same.

A few examples: "As always", "Onward & Upwards!", "Consider it done"... The possibilities are endless.

***

Lastly, always know that e-mail is the best way to reach influencers.

Today, most people hardly ever pick up the phone, *but* they read their e-mails on their smart-phones all day long, even before and after work hours.

If you send an e-mail around 6:30 a.m., chances are your recipient reads it even before they arrive at the office.

~ * ~

THANK YOU for buying
NAKED WORDS 2.0 The Effective 157-Word Email

Please leave a review at Amazon.com – i value your opinion tremendously. Thank-You!
www.amazon.com/Gisela-Hausmann/e/B000APN192

To find out about upcoming "naked books" and other noteworthy news, please subscribe at
www.giselahausmann.com/free-creative-ideas.html

I value and respect subscribers and will not inundate you with sales e-mails.

As always,
Gisela Hausmann

More books:

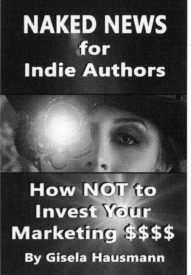

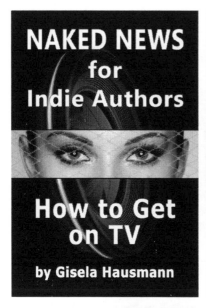

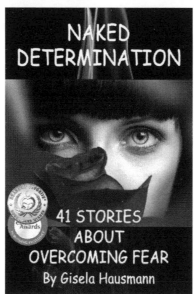

Notes:

Notes:

Notes:

Made in the USA
Lexington, KY
23 March 2017